If I Were a
Veterinarian

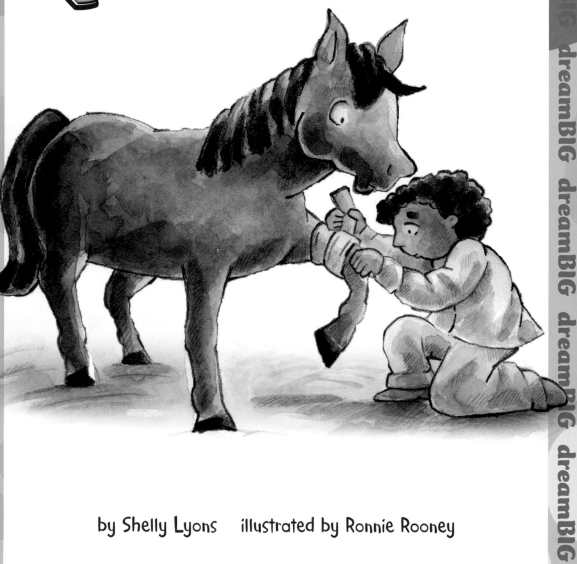

by Shelly Lyons   illustrated by Ronnie Rooney

Special thanks to our advisers for their expertise:

Luci T. Dimick, DVM, Assistant Professor - Clinical
Ohio State University, Columbus, Ohio

Terry Flaherty, PhD, Professor of English
Minnesota State University, Mankato

PICTURE WINDOW BOOKS
a capstone imprint

Editor: Jill Kalz
Designer: Tracy Davies
Art Director: Nathan Gassman
Production Specialist: Jane Klenk

The illustrations in this book were created with watercolor and colored pencil.

Picture Window Books
151 Good Counsel Drive
P.O. Box 669
Mankato, MN 56002-0669
877-845-8392
www.capstonepub.com

Library of Congress Cataloging-in-Publication Data
Lyons, Shelly.
   If I were a veterinarian / by Shelly Lyons ; illustrated by
Ronnie Rooney.
       p. cm. — (Dream big!)
   Includes index.
   ISBN 978-1-4048-6161-9 (library binding)
   ISBN 978-1-4048-6399-6 (paperback)
   1. Veterinarians—Vocational guidance—Juvenile literature.
I. Rooney, Ronnie, ill. II. Title.
   SF756.28.L96 2011
   636.089092—dc22
                                    2010000896

Printed in the United States of America in North Mankato, Minnesota.
012011   006057R

If I were a veterinarian, my patients would purr, hiss, or bark.

If I were a veterinarian, I would be an animal doctor. I would be called a vet for short.

Most of the time, I would work in a veterinary clinic. But sometimes I would visit farms, zoos, or even the circus!

6

If I were a vet, I would take a peek inside a puppy's ears and mouth. I would listen to its heart thump. I would tell the puppy's owner how to care for her new pet. I would also help her sign up for puppy training classes.

If I were a vet, I would check a cat from head to toe. I would look for cuts, scrapes, and little spots that hurt. A shot would help keep the cat healthy.

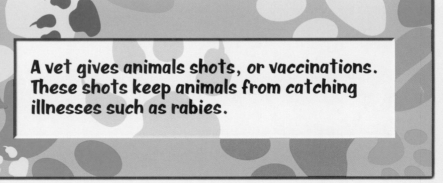

A vet gives animals shots, or vaccinations. These shots keep animals from catching illnesses such as rabies.

If I were a vet, I would ask a pet rat to say CHEESE! An X-ray machine would take pictures of the animal's insides. I would study the pictures for broken bones.

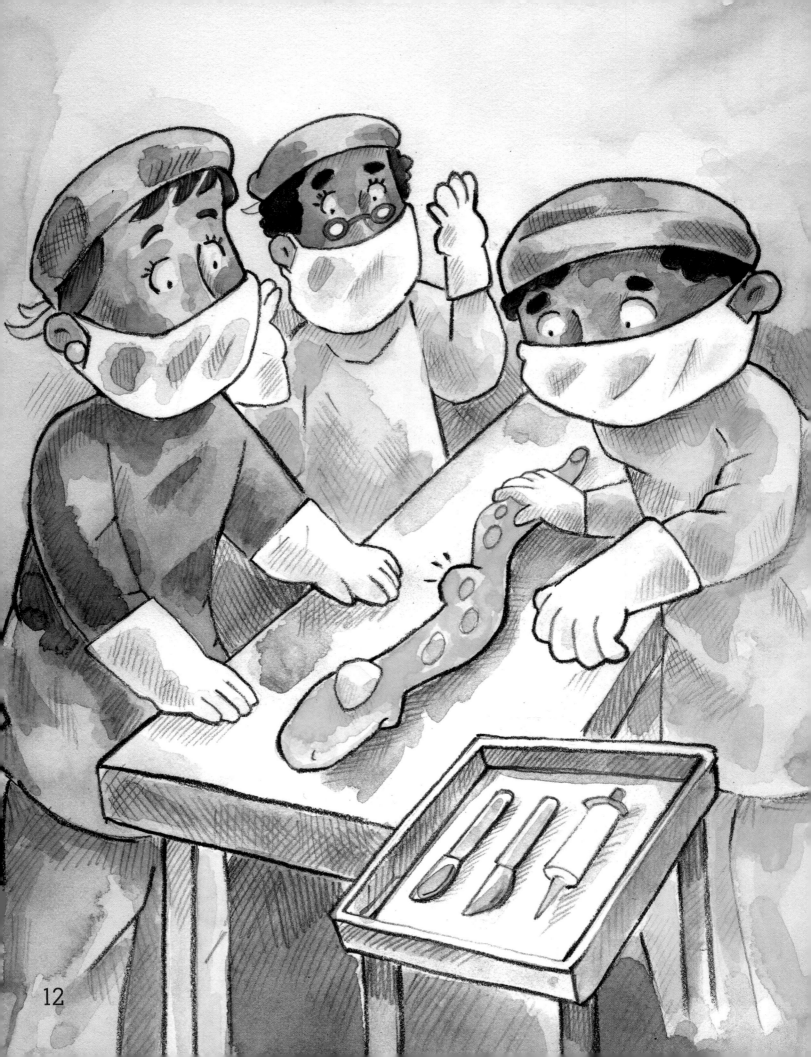

If I were a vet, I would remove a swallowed golf ball from a snake. A team of people would help me operate.

Before an operation, a vet gives the animal a shot of special medicine. The shot sedates the animal. Then the vet uses tools, such as a scalpel, to cut into the animal's skin.

If I were a vet, I would help pet owners make tough decisions. People are sad when their pets get very sick or very old. I would help owners do what's best for their pets.

If I were a vet, I would work day or night. I would race to a local farm on an emergency call. I would bring my vet box. I would stitch and bandage a horse's leg.

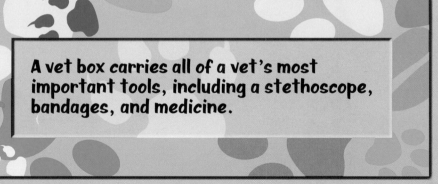

A vet box carries all of a vet's most important tools, including a stethoscope, bandages, and medicine.

If I were a vet, I might be called to the zoo. I would sedate a tiger. Then I would fix the tiger's aching tooth. But I would have to work very quickly!

If I were a vet, I would love taking care of all kinds of animals. People would look to me to keep their pets healthy.

How do you get to be a

Veterinarian ?

You must really like animals and do well in science and math to become a veterinarian. After graduating from college, you need to go to a school of veterinary medicine. It takes four years to finish those classes. At graduation, you are given a Doctor of Veterinary Medicine (DVM or VMD) degree.

After getting your degree, you will need to pass a licensing test. A license gives you permission to be a veterinarian. Many new vets also practice, or intern, with other vets for about a year. Vets continue to take classes every year to keep their skills sharp.

Vets may choose to work in just one area. For example, vet specialists may treat only small animals or only animals' teeth. They may focus on heart disease, behavior problems, animal surgery, or emergency care.

Glossary

degree—a title given to a person for finishing a course of study in college

license—a paper, or document, that gives permission to do something

patient—someone who is taken care of by a doctor

rabies—a deadly disease spread by animal bites

scalpel—a small, sharp knife used to cut skin

sedate—to give a drug to make a person or animal sleep for a time

vaccination—a shot of medicine that protects people or animals from disease

veterinary clinic—a place where veterinarians care for animals

To Learn More

More Books to Read

Adamson, Heather. *A Day in the Life of a Veterinarian.* Community Helpers at Work. Mankato, Minn.: Capstone Press, 2004.

Jackson, Donna M. *ER Vets: Life in an Animal Emergency Room.* Boston: Houghton Mifflin, 2005.

Parks, Peggy J. *Veterinarian.* Exploring Careers. San Diego: Kidhaven Press, 2004.

Thomas, William David. *Veterinarian.* Pleasantville, N.Y.: Gareth Stevens Pub., 2009.

Internet Sites

FactHound offers a safe, fun way to find Internet sites related to this book. All of the sites on FactHound have been researched by our staff.

Here's all you do:

Visit *www.facthound.com*

FactHound will fetch the best sites for you!

Index

Look for all of the books in the Dream Big! series:

If I Were a Ballerina
If I Were a Cowboy
If I Were a Firefighter
If I Were a Major League Baseball Player
If I Were a Movie Star
If I Were a Veterinarian
If I Were an Astronaut
If I Were the President